Baseball Players Do Amazing Things

by Mel Cebulash

Illustrated with photographs

Step-Up Books   Random House

New York

Photograph credits: Culver Pictures, front endpaper; Ken Regan, 51; United Press, 8, 14, 15, 19, 20, 22, 23, 28, 33, 36, 38, 39 (right), 40, 42, 43, 48, 54, 56, 60, 62, 65, 68; Wide World, 12, 17, 21, 25, 27, 31, 34, 39 (left), 45, 47, 52, 53, 58, 63, 66, back endpaper.
Cover: photo by Tony Triolo for *Sports Illustrated* © Time Inc.

Library of Congress Cataloging in Publication Data Cebulash, Mel. Baseball players do amazing things. (Step-up books) 1. Baseball—Juvenile literature. I. Title. GV867.5.C42 1973 796.357 72-11272 ISBN 0-394-82611-6 ISBN 0-394-92611-0 (lib. bdg.)

Manufactured in the United States of America

CONTENTS

Oriole catcher Elrod Hendricks tags Bernie Carbo.
But the ball is not in his glove!

Going for Home

October 10, 1970. The first game of the World Series was being played in Cincinnati. The Reds were playing the Baltimore Orioles.

After five innings, the score was 3–3. The Orioles didn't get any runs in the sixth. Then the Reds came to bat, and their Cincinnati fans cheered.

One Red batter struck out. Then Bernie Carbo was walked. The next Red up got a one-base hit. Carbo used this hit to move to third base. Again, the Cincinnati fans cheered. They hoped that the next batter would bring Carbo home.

The next batter hit the ball slowly toward third. Ellie Hendricks, the Orioles' catcher, went after the ball. The umpire behind the plate ran up the line after Hendricks. He wanted to make sure the ball was a fair one.

At the same time, Bernie Carbo started down the line. He was running hard for home.

The Oriole catcher got the ball and turned fast. He turned right into the umpire and knocked him down!

Bernie Carbo began to slide into home. But the umpire was on the ground, right in his way. Carbo tried to slide around the umpire. But he missed home plate.

At the same time the Oriole catcher was trying to get Carbo out. He tagged the Cincinnati runner with his glove hand. But the ball was in his throwing hand! The catcher missed the runner, and the runner missed the plate!

The umpire got a quick look at what was happening and called Carbo out. The Cincinnati fans thought Carbo was safe. But the umpire would not change his mind.

In the next inning, Baltimore scored a run and won the game, 4–3.

If Carbo had scored in the sixth, the game would have ended with some other score. But no one can be sure Cincinnati would have won. No one ever knows what will happen next in a baseball game!

The stories in this book will show you why.

The Babe Hits One

Baseball fans still talk about "Babe" Ruth. His real name was George Herman Ruth. But when he started playing, he looked very young. The other players all called him "Babe." And the name stayed with him for the rest of his life.

As a baseball player, Babe Ruth did many great things. But he is remembered most for his home runs. He hit over 700 of them. This is the story of one of his most famous hits.

In 1932, Babe was playing for the New York Yankees. On October 1, his team played against the Chicago Cubs at Chicago's field.

It was the third game of the World Series.

In the fifth inning, Babe went up to bat. His team had four runs, and the Cubs had four. Charlie Root was pitching for the Cubs. He was a very good pitcher.

Charlie's first pitch came in. It was a strike. Babe held up a finger. "That's one," he said.

Another pitch came in. It was a ball. Babe held up two fingers. Root threw two more times. The count rose to two strikes and two balls.

Then Babe waved at the fence. He was telling the pitcher that he was going to hit the next throw over the fence. He was telling everybody that he was going to hit a home run.

The people watching the game could not believe their eyes. Many of them laughed. Did Babe Ruth think he was that great? Could he be so sure he was going to hit the next throw over the fence?

Everybody watched closely while

Charlie Root got ready to throw. The pitch came in. Babe Ruth swung. His bat hit the ball—hard! He started for first base. The ball flew high over the fence. It was a home run!

15

He had said he was going to hit a home run. And he had hit one.

As Babe went around the bases, he laughed. He had pointed to the fence. And that was where the ball had gone.

In the stands, the fans went wild, cheering.

Dizzy
Dean

Paul
Dean

The Dean Brothers

Dizzy and Paul Dean were brothers.
And they both pitched for the St.
Louis Cardinals. They also liked to do
crazy things—both on and off the
baseball field.

Dizzy's real name was Jerome. But
he was known as Dizzy to the other
players and the fans. They said that
batters got dizzy swinging at his fast
ball. Paul was often called Daffy.

17

Dizzy was the older brother. And he often pitched better than Paul. But not all the time.

On September 21, 1934, the Cardinals had two games to play. Both games were against the Brooklyn Dodgers in Brooklyn.

Dizzy Dean pitched the first game for the Cardinals. And he pitched a very good game. He gave up only two hits. It was an easy win for Dizzy. Even the Brooklyn fans cheered him.

Dizzy didn't leave after his game. He wanted to watch his younger brother pitch.

While Dizzy watched, Paul started the second game. In the first inning, the Dodgers didn't get a hit off Paul.

Dizzy's younger brother stopped the

Dodgers without a hit in the second inning, too. He was off to a good start.

Inning after inning, the Dodgers didn't get a hit. At the end of the eighth inning, the fans clapped hard for Paul. He needed only three more outs for a no-hitter.

The Dodgers tried very hard in the ninth. They wanted to win. But no one could get a hit off Paul that day. The fans stood and cheered. Paul Dean had done better than his brother. He had pitched a no-hitter!

Dizzy was happy for his brother. He hugged him, while other players gathered around to tell Paul how well he had pitched.

Then Dizzy said, "Paul, why didn't you tell me you were going to pitch a no-hitter? I'd have done it, too!"

The players laughed. Only Dizzy Dean could say things like that!

Joe Medwick

The Day the Fans Went Wild

October 9, 1934. The Detroit Tigers and St. Louis Cardinals were playing the seventh and last game of the World Series.

It was a big day for the people of Detroit. They filled the ball park. They hoped their Tigers would win the game and become world champions.

But in the third inning, the Cardinals scored seven runs. Now the Detroit fans knew that their team didn't have much of a chance. Still they hated to see the championship go to St. Louis.

21

During the sixth inning trouble started. Joe Medwick, a St. Louis outfielder, was running for third base. He slid right into Marvin Owen, Detroit's third baseman. Medwick hoped to knock the ball out of Owen's hand. But Owen held on to it.

The two men got into a fight. It was stopped quickly. But the Detroit fans didn't like what they had seen. They were angry at Medwick. They were angry, too, because their team was losing.

When the Cardinals finished their turn at bat, Medwick went out to the field. The Detroit fans were waiting for him. Fruit, vegetables, and other things came sailing out of the stands.

The fans went wild. Joe Medwick was in real trouble!

The game stopped for a while. Then it started again. But the Detroit fans would not leave Medwick alone. What could be done? The commissioner of baseball had to answer that question. He was in charge.

The commissioner asked that Joe be taken out. He thought the game should go on. But he did not want Medwick to get hurt.

St. Louis finally won the game, 11–0. The Cardinals became the 1934 world champions.

The Detroit fans went home feeling very sad that day. Their team had lost. And they had acted like very poor sports.

Joe Medwick leaves the field.

Joe Medwick, on the other hand, could feel very happy. He had led the Cardinals in batting. And he had become the first and only player taken out of a Series game for his safety!

The Smallest Man Ever to Play

The little man's name was Eddie Gaedel. He was 26 years old, but only 43 inches tall. Eddie Gaedel was a midget.

The St. Louis Browns put Eddie on their team for a joke. They did not tell anyone what they were doing. They wanted it to be a surprise.

The Browns knew everyone would talk about Eddie. There would be stories about him in the newspapers. This might bring more people to watch their games.

On August 18, 1951, Eddie played in his first game. The Browns sent him to bat in the first inning. He

had a very small bat in his hands. It
was really a toy bat. But Eddie didn't
plan to hit any baseballs. He had
orders to let the pitches go by.

The Detroit players stared at Eddie. They did not believe that he could really be a Brown player. But they soon found out that they were wrong. The little man stood at the plate, ready to bat.

The Detroit pitcher did not know how to throw to such a short player. He tried to get a strike on his first pitch. But the ball flew over Eddie's head.

Bob Caen, the Detroit pitcher.

The pitcher tried again. And once more the baseball sailed over Eddie's head. It was ball two.

The Detroit pitcher started laughing. He knew there was just no way to pitch to little Eddie Gaedel. But he threw the ball two more times. His throws were so low the catcher had to get on his knees. But still the ball sailed way over the little batter's head.

Eddie had a walk. He dropped his bat and headed for first base.

Then St. Louis sent a man to first to run for Eddie. And Eddie left the field.

The fans were all laughing. The St. Louis team had certainly thought of a funny stunt. Eddie was laughing, too. But he knew it was not fair.

He could get on base every time he came to bat. No pitcher could throw a strike to him.

But Eddie was sure the fun would not last, and he was right. The next day a special rule was made. St. Louis could not have a midget on its team. No team could have a midget playing for it.

So Eddie Gaedel became the smallest man ever to play on a big-league team. He will probably always hold that record.

The Amazing Willie Mays

Some players can hit. Some players can run. Some players can field. Few players can do all three things. But Willie Mays could do them—and well.

Stories about Willie Mays could fill a book. This is one of them.

Willie was with the Giants in 1954. On September 29 they met the Cleveland Indians in the first game of the World Series. The game was played on the Giants' field.

After seven innings, the score was 2–2. Then the Indians got off to a good start in the eighth. The first two men at bat got on base.

The next Indian batter was Vic Wertz. He was a good hitter. It looked as if the Indians would score again.

The runners on first and second got ready. But, with no outs, they had to be careful.

Then Wertz hit the ball—up and

Vic Wertz takes a swing.

away! It flew far out into center field.
It seemed to be way over Willie Mays'
head.

But Willie turned and started for
the ball. He ran hard and fast. He
seemed to know just where the ball
was going.

As it started to come down, Willie looked up over his shoulder. He put his hands out in front of him, ready to catch. The ball dropped into his glove, like an apple falling into a basket. Wertz was out!

Willie stopped fast. He turned and

threw the ball to the infield. The runners hurried back to their bases.

The fans stood and cheered. Some said it was the greatest catch ever made. It may have been. Anyway, it was the kind of catch that only Willie Mays could make!

After Willie's catch, the Indians did not score in the eighth inning. And the game was still tied, 2–2, after the ninth. The two teams had to play an extra inning.

At last the Giants scored three more runs and won the game, 5–2.

The three runs won the game. But everybody said that Willie Mays' catch had made it possible. He had stopped the Indians when everybody was sure they would score.

After 18 Years

May 2, 1954—a double-header in St. Louis. The Cardinals were playing two games against the Giants.

The Cardinals' greatest star was Stan Musial. And on that day in May he played better than ever.

In the first game, Stan Musial hit three home runs. The St. Louis fans cheered and cheered. It isn't often that a player hits three home runs in a game.

But Stan Musial wasn't ready to stop. He hit two more home runs in the second game. This time the St. Louis fans stood up and clapped. Eight-year-old Nate Colbert stood with them. He had just seen the great Stan Musial hit five home runs! It was a thrill for little Nate Colbert. And it was a new record for Stan Musial.

―――――

July 31, 1972—a double-header in Atlanta. The San Diego Padres were playing two games against the Braves.

It was the ninth inning of the second game. San Diego's big first baseman came to the plate. He got ready to hit.

The pitch came in, and the big first baseman hit it hard. The ball sailed high over the left field fence. It was a home run!

Nate Colbert batting for San Diego.

As the big first baseman ran the bases, everyone in the stands began to cheer. Then they stood and clapped.

The 26-year-old first baseman had tied Stan Musial's record. He had hit two home runs in the first game and three home runs in the second game. He had hit five home runs in a double-header.

The San Diego first baseman was pleased with himself. He should have been. As little Nate Colbert, he had watched Stan Musial's five home runs. As big Nate Colbert, he had just hit five home runs of his own!

The Amazing Jackie Robinson

September 28, 1955. The Dodgers were playing the Yankees in the World Series. At the end of seven innings, the Yankees were ahead, 6–3.

The Dodgers came up to bat at the start of the eighth inning. Their fans began clapping. They wanted the Dodgers to get some more runs.

Carl Furillo, the first batter, got a hit. But the next batter made an out. Then the great Jackie Robinson came to bat. The Dodger fans cheered. Jackie could help get them some of the runs they needed.

Seconds later, Jackie hit a ball that looked like an easy out. But a Yankee fielder made a bad throw.

Carl Furillo at bat.

When the play was over, Jackie Robinson was on second base. Carl Furillo was on third. And the Dodgers' fans were clapping and cheering.

The next Dodger hit a long fly to the outfield. A Yankee fielder caught it, but Furillo raced home. Jackie Robinson moved over to third base.

Now the Dodgers had four runs to the Yankees' six. The Dodgers also had two outs.

The Yankee pitcher, Whitey Ford,

looked at the next Dodger batter. Then he looked over at third base. It isn't easy to steal home. But Ford knew that Robinson could do it.

Yogi Berra, the Yankee catcher, also looked down the line at Robinson. Then Berra got ready for the throw. The pitch came in. It was outside for a ball.

Yankee Whitey Ford pitching.

Again, the Yankee pitcher and catcher looked at Robinson. He knew they were watching him. The Dodger fans were watching, too. They wondered if Robinson would take a chance. Would he try to steal home?

Whitey Ford got ready. He started his pitching move. Right away Jackie Robinson started running. He was racing for home plate against Whitey Ford's pitch!

Everybody in the stands started to cheer. It was going to be a close play.

Before the ball reached Yogi Berra's glove, Jackie started his slide into home. Then Berra caught the ball.

It was too late! Robinson's foot had touched home plate. He was "safe." He had stolen home!

Berra wasn't happy. He thought he had gotten Robinson in time. But there was nothing Berra could do about it. The umpire said that Robinson was "safe."

Yankee fans went home happy that day. The Yankees won the game, 6–5. But the Dodger fans went home happy, too. They had seen the great Jackie Robinson make one of the most amazing steals ever in a World Series game.

Harvey Haddix

The Greatest Game Ever Pitched

May 26, 1959. The Pittsburgh Pirates were playing the Braves at Milwaukee. It was a cool night, and the Pirates had picked Harvey Haddix to pitch. Haddix was small for a pitcher. And at age 33, he was nearing the end of his playing days.

After one inning, the score was 0–0. Harvey Haddix had faced three Braves. And the little left-hander had gotten three Braves out.

At the end of six innings, the Braves still had no hits. Harvey Haddix hadn't even walked a man. Through six innings, he had pitched a perfect no-hit game!

In the seventh, the Braves went down again—one, two, three. Haddix still had his perfect game going. The people in the stands were very quiet. So were the players.

In the eighth, the Braves again went down one, two, three. Haddix was now three outs away from a perfect no-hit game. Not one Brave had gotten to first base.

But the Pirates had not gotten a run either. The score was 0–0. The Pirates needed at least one run to win.

Harvey Haddix went out for the ninth. He knew he could still lose his no-hitter—and the game. He pitched hard, and once more the Braves went down in order. The people in the stands cheered.

After nine innings, the score was still 0–0. The game moved into extra innings. But the Pirates still could not get the one run they needed.

For three more innings, little Harvey Haddix pitched perfect ball. He had faced 36 men and had gotten 36 men out! It was the greatest game ever pitched. But how long could he last?

Even the Milwaukee fans wished the Pirates would get a run in the thirteenth inning. But still the Pirates did not score.

Harvey Haddix went out for the bottom of the thirteenth. By this time he was tired. His left arm began to hurt. But he hoped he could keep pitching until his team got a run.

The first Brave at bat hit a ball to third. The throw went to first. It was a bad throw! The man was safe. Harvey's perfect game was over after twelve innings.

The next batter bunted for an out. But the man on first moved over to second.

The great Henry Aaron was the next batter. A hit by Aaron could end the game! Aaron was a strong hitter. Haddix threw four balls to Aaron and let him walk to first.

Hank Aaron at bat for Milwaukee.

Haddix hoped to get the next batter to hit the ball on the ground. He hoped his Pirates could get a double play. Then the inning would be over.

But Joe Adcock, the next batter, wanted to get a hit. And he did! A two-base hit. The man on second raced around the bases and stepped on home. The game was over. The Braves had won it, 1–0.

Joe Adcock in the locker room.

A happy Harvey Haddix.

The people in the stands cheered Harvey Haddix as he walked off the field. He had pitched 12 perfect, no-hit innings. He had pitched the greatest game ever. And then—at the very end—he had lost it.

His 100th Home Run

In 1963 Jimmy Piersall was playing for the New York Mets. On June 23 he came up to bat in a game against the Philadelphia Phillies. He hit the ball. It flew over the fence and out of the park.

He had hit a home run!

But it was more than just a home run. It was his 100th homer in the big leagues.

Jimmy was so happy that he decided to do something funny. He started for first base running backward.

Soon Jimmy reached first base and went on to second. He was still running backward! The Philadelphia players were surprised. So were the people in the stands.

In fact, everybody was surprised except Jimmy Piersall.

Running backward, he touched second, third, and home. He had scored a run for the Mets.

The people in the stands clapped and laughed. They had never seen anybody run the bases backward.

And they would never see such a thing again.

Soon after Jimmy's surprising run, the home-run rule was changed. Now, when a man hits a home run, he must go around the bases. He must touch every base. But he must also *face* the bases. He has to run forward. If he runs backward, he is out.

Jimmy Piersall was not the first player to hit 100 home runs. But he may have been the first player to get a home run while running backward.

He will also be the last!

The
All-Around
Player

September 22, 1968. The Minnesota
Twins were playing the Oakland
Athletics. The starting pitcher for the
Twins was Cesar Tovar.

Most of the time Cesar was an
outfielder. Sometimes he was an
infielder. But for this game he was
going to try to play every position.

The people in the stands watched Cesar's practice pitches. "He won't get through the inning," many thought. "He's too little!"

The first Athletic came to bat. Cesar got him out. Then he struck out the second batter. The third batter walked. But the next batter was put out. Cesar had pitched the first inning. And he had not given any runs to the Athletics.

In the second inning, Cesar played catcher for the Twins. Again, many people thought, "He's too little!" But 150-pound Cesar fooled them. He played well.

Tovar moved to first base in the third inning. Again, he played well and got through the inning.

Cesar also batted against the Athletics.

After that, Cesar moved to a new spot every inning. At the end of the game, he had played everywhere!

The fans clapped as he ran off the field. Cesar Tovar had shown that he was a true all-around player!

No Help Needed

July 30, 1968. The Cleveland Indians were playing the Washington Senators. The game was at night on the Cleveland field.

The score was still 0–0 when the Indians came to bat in the first inning. They wanted to get some hits. Most of the people watching the game were Cleveland fans. They wanted the Indians to get some runs, too.

The Cleveland team wasted no time. Its first two batters both got on base. The people in the stands began to cheer. Now their team had men on first and second base. And there were no outs. The Washington Senators were in trouble.

Jose Azcue

Cleveland's third batter, Jose Azcue, stepped up to the plate. All the Washington players were in place on the field. They were watching carefully. They could not let the Indians get another hit.

Their shortstop, Ron Hansen, stood between second and third base. He slapped his glove. He also watched the Indian runners on first and second base. If the ball came his way, he

Ron Hansen

might be able to stop them.

Azcue, the Indians' batter, got three balls and two strikes. If the next pitch was over the plate, the Senators knew he would swing.

When the pitcher threw the ball, the Indians on first and second started running. It was a good pitch. Azcue swung. He hit the ball hard. It went straight through the air toward Ron Hansen.

Hansen caught the ball. Azcue was out.

Quickly Ron ran to second base. He touched it before the runner could get back. That made two outs.

By this time the runner from first base had almost reached second. He tried to stop so he could run back to first. He was too late. Ron reached out and tagged him.

In only a few seconds Hansen had gotten three players out. All by himself he had made a triple play. The Washington team was out of trouble.

In the big leagues a triple play doesn't often happen. A triple play *by one man* almost never happens. Ron Hansen was the first player in

**A smiling Ron Hansen leaves
the locker room after the game.**

forty years to make a triple play all
by himself.

Even though Ron was playing for
the Washington Senators, the Cleveland
fans clapped when he walked off the
field. His amazing play deserved their
cheers.

A Second Try

In 1969 Carlos May played his first
full year in the big leagues. He played
in the outfield for the Chicago White
Sox. And he played very well.

By August, Carlos was one of the
stars of the team. He had over 100
hits, and 18 of them were home runs.

Then Carlos had to leave the team. He had to go to Marine training camp in California. But it was for only a short time. He would be back.

Then something happened to change Carlos' plans. He was hurt at training camp. A shell went off in his right hand. He lost part of the thumb on his throwing hand!

The White Sox got the bad news first. Then baseball fans all over the United States read it in their papers.

The Chicago fans were the unhappiest. They liked young Carlos May. And they felt sorry to think that his playing days were over.

Carlos stayed in the hospital for a long time. Doctors worked on his thumb. They did the best they could.

But the doctors knew Carlos' thumb would never be the same. And they couldn't say for sure if he would ever play again.

In the spring of 1970, Carlos came out to try to play again. Baseball fans hoped that he would make it. But they were afraid he didn't have much of a chance. Baseball isn't an easy game, even with two good thumbs.

Carlos surprised the team and the fans. No one needed to feel sorry for him. He tried hard and played well. He not only got back on the team. He also won back his starting place in the outfield. And he batted better than he had the year before!

Carlos might have given up after he hurt his thumb. It would have been easy to quit. But he wanted to play baseball. He was willing to make a second try. And he showed that a good man doesn't let even big things get him down.